SHOCK ZONE™
GAMES AND GAMERS

THE WILD WORLD OF GAMING CULTURE

ARIE KAPLAN

Lerner Publications Company • Minneapolis

NOTE TO READERS: Not all games are appropriate for players of all ages. Remember to follow video game rating systems and the advice of a parent or guardian when deciding which games to play.

Lerner Publications Company
A division of Lerner Publishing Group, Inc.
241 First Avenue North
Minneapolis, MN 55401 U.S.A.

Website address: www.lernerbooks.com

Content Consultant: Crystle Martin, postdoctoral researcher, Digital Media and Learning Hub at the University of California, Irvine

Library of Congress Cataloging-in-Publication Data

The Cataloging-in-Publication Data for *The Wild World of Gaming Culture* is on file at the Library of Congress.
ISBN 978–1–4677–1252–1 (LB)
ISBN 978–1–4677–1784–7 (EB)

Manufactured in the United States of America
1 — MG — 7/15/13

TABLE OF
CONTENTS

The world of video games is filled with millions of colorful, creative, and passionate characters that are always ready for action. **And those are just the fans.**

When you think about video games, you should think about more than just the games and their creators. You should also consider the huge number of things those games inspire. This includes books, movies,

TV shows, and more. For big fans of gaming, it can influence things in their everyday lives, including whom they play games with, what they read and write, and even how they dress. There's no question about it—gaming culture is bigger now than it has ever been before. But what exactly is gaming culture?

For a long time, people have thought of gaming as something for lonely nerds playing in their parents' basements, sipping on cola, and eating handfuls of chips. But this couldn't be further from the truth. There are a million ways to play games socially, whether it's with your best friends or with total strangers. And when people game together, they instantly have something in common. Gamers of all kinds hang out and talk with one another in person and online, bonding over their shared experiences and discussing the wild world of gaming culture.

Stay safe while gaming. Don't give out your personal information online.

MULTIPLAYER GAMING:
Real Friends, Virtual Worlds

It used to be that the only way to play games with your friends was to invite them over to your house. Players had to have their own controllers and plug them into the console. And then the screen would be split depending on how many people were playing. Playing a four-person game? The screen would be split into four parts. Good luck seeing anything.

But that's all changed in recent years. Online gaming has become the number one way to play. When people hook up their console or computer to the Internet, they can play with anyone in the world at any time. With this much freedom, it's no wonder that the online gaming culture grew quickly.

People who enjoy playing the same game together began forming groups called guilds or clans. They often keep schedules, carving out a set amount of time in their week to play together. Many times, members of these groups become friends outside the game too. But even though they might never meet in person, they get to know one another quite well through the game. Because of this, guilds can sometimes feel like families.

guilds = groups of gamers that play online together regularly

BRINGING ONLINE GAMING TO CONSOLES

Console games have been played online since the mid-1990s, but early ways of playing were experimental and never became popular. It wasn't until the launch of Xbox Live in 2002 that online console gaming really hit the mainstream. Xbox Live made it easy for gamers to find their friends online, send them messages, and even voice chat during games. By 2012 there were more than 40 million Xbox Live subscribers worldwide.

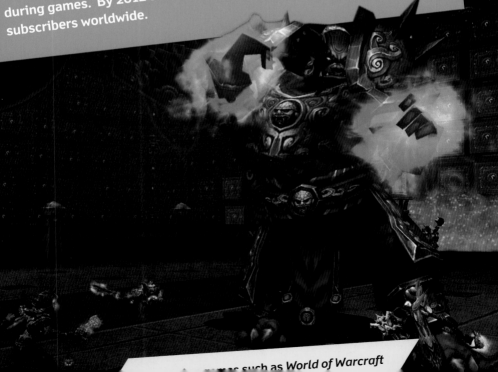

... games such as *World of Warcraft*

Playing in the same room gives players a chance to meet people face-to-face between games.

With the release of Xbox Live, online gaming had become more popular than playing multiplayer games on a single console. But another way of playing with friends combines the best parts of these two forms of gaming. This style of multiplayer is known as local area network (LAN) gaming.

LAN gamers usually play in the same room. But just like with online gaming, they each use their own computer or console and screen. They connect their computers or consoles into a local network rather than to the Internet. This means that the game never slows down due to a slow Internet connection. LAN gamers also don't have to worry about split screens when playing with others.

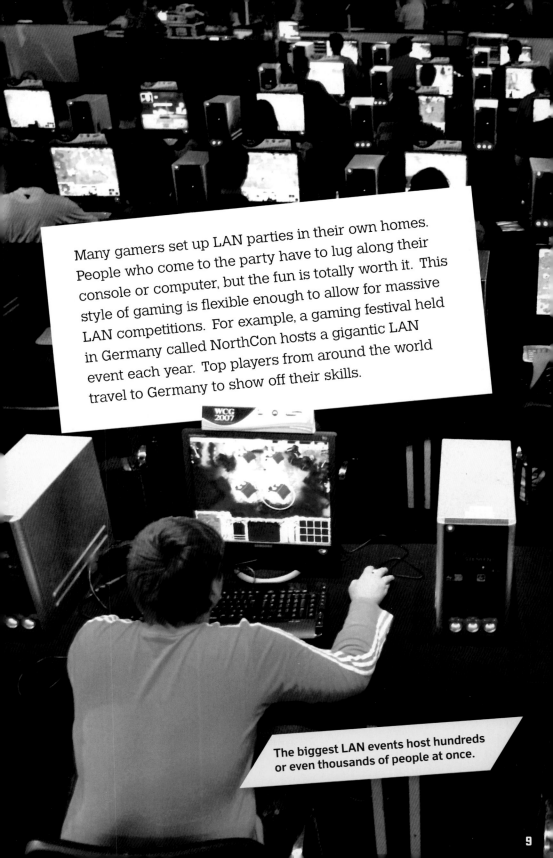

Many gamers set up LAN parties in their own homes. People who come to the party have to lug along their console or computer, but the fun is totally worth it. This style of gaming is flexible enough to allow for massive LAN competitions. For example, a gaming festival held in Germany called NorthCon hosts a gigantic LAN event each year. Top players from around the world travel to Germany to show off their skills.

The biggest LAN events host hundreds or even thousands of people at once.

VIDEO GAME COMPETITIONS:
Gaming for Cash

Why do people love playing video games? Fun, excitement, and friendship are all great reasons. But there's one more benefit of being a skilled gamer: cold, hard cash.

Many of the world's top gamers earn their living playing in video game tournaments. Huge cash prizes are at stake for players who can dominate in games like *Halo* and *Call of Duty*. The matches are sometimes even shown on huge screens so that a crowd of fans can follow the action. If a professional gamer becomes popular with fans, he or she can even get endorsement deals from companies that make gaming gear.

endorsement deals = getting paid money to promote a particular product

However, being a professional gamer isn't easy. You need tons of discipline to practice for hours every day. You've got to consistently play against skilled opponents, because that's the best way to improve. It can be very stressful to spend so much time playing, so it's helpful for pro gamers to be part of a gaming community that knows what they're going through and that will support them. Major League Gaming (MLG), one of the largest professional gaming leagues, holds major events and gives pro gamers a chance to socialize with one another.

Gaming competitions have become fairly popular in the United States but nowhere near as popular as in South Korea. The strategy game *StarCraft* and its sequel, *StarCraft II*, have practically become national sports in the East Asian nation. Matches have been shown on TV, and thousands of people attend the top tournaments. The top prize for a recent *StarCraft II* tournament in South Korea was $100,000.

Professional gamer Moon Sung Won plays *Starcraft II* in a tournament in 2011.

VIDEO GAME TRADE SHOWS:
Showing Off

Imagine walking into a vast convention center. Bright lights and loud noises overwhelm you as you look around the room. You're surrounded by displays showing every major video game that will come out over the next year. Games are being shown on giant screens. Video game designers are talking to fans, and people are walking around dressed as game characters. What is this place? You've found yourself at a video game trade show.

video game designers = people who create video games

Trade shows give the video game industry a major chance to show off. New games and systems are announced at trade shows, and companies give away tons of free stuff. It's all done to help raise awareness and excitement for the industry's latest and greatest products. It's a gamer's paradise.

One of the biggest trade shows is the Electronic Entertainment Expo, or E3. The show was first held way back in 1995. E3 attracts game companies of all sizes. Unfortunately, the general public is not allowed to attend. The trade show is open only to game-industry professionals—mostly game creators and game journalists. Still, millions of gamers love to follow the breaking news at E3 from their favorite news sources.

Other trade shows, including Gamescom in Germany and the Tokyo Game Show in Japan, allow the general public inside the show. These events give gamers an exciting chance to go hands-on with games that might not show up in stores for a year or more.

THE FIRST E3
A huge selection of new video game consoles were discussed at the first E3 in 1995, but only one of them would prove successful. The Sega Saturn, the Atari Jaguar VR, the Nintendo Virtual Boy, the 3DO M2, and the SNK Neo-Geo CD were all talked about at the show. Each was discontinued within a few years, if it was released at all. The lone successful system was the Sony PlayStation.

E3 is often held at the massive Los Angeles Convention Center.

FAN FICTION:
Expanding the Universe

You've just finished your favorite game of all time. You loved the characters, the graphics, and the story—but now it's all over. And there's no sequel planned. What are you going to do?

For some creative gamers, the answer is fan fiction. Many video game fans love the fictional worlds of their favorite games so much that they wish those worlds could continue on forever, well after they finish playing the game. They write stories and create movies that let people revisit the characters and situations players loved.

Fan fiction has been around for a long time for TV shows such as *Star Trek* and novels such as *The Lord of the Rings*. It's not too surprising that the richly imagined fantasy worlds of video games have also inspired creative fans. There is fan fiction devoted to a wide range of games, from *Halo* to *The Legend of Zelda* and beyond.

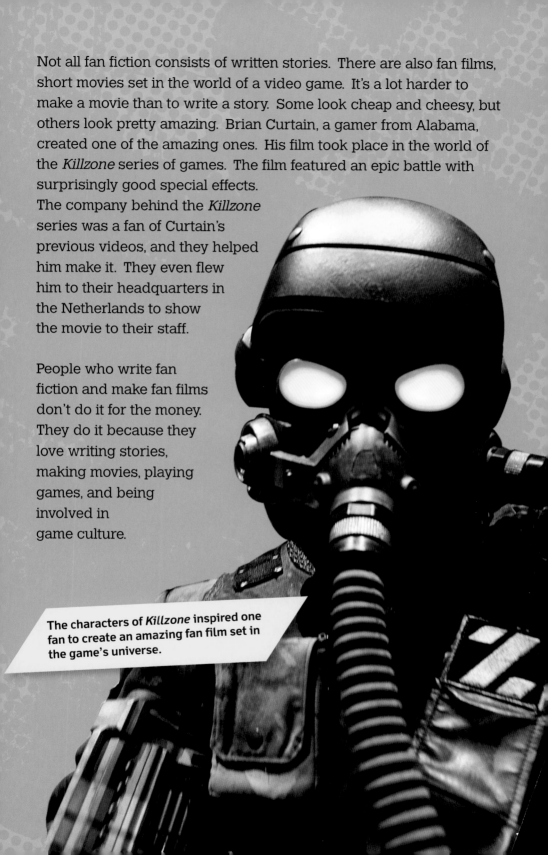

Not all fan fiction consists of written stories. There are also fan films, short movies set in the world of a video game. It's a lot harder to make a movie than to write a story. Some look cheap and cheesy, but others look pretty amazing. Brian Curtain, a gamer from Alabama, created one of the amazing ones. His film took place in the world of the *Killzone* series of games. The film featured an epic battle with surprisingly good special effects. The company behind the *Killzone* series was a fan of Curtain's previous videos, and they helped him make it. They even flew him to their headquarters in the Netherlands to show the movie to their staff.

People who write fan fiction and make fan films don't do it for the money. They do it because they love writing stories, making movies, playing games, and being involved in game culture.

The characters of *Killzone* inspired one fan to create an amazing fan film set in the game's universe.

COSPLAY:
Dressed to Impress

Have you ever wanted to put on the armor of a super soldier from space?

Swing the sword of an epic hero? Or just wear Mario's overalls and hat? Then maybe you should get into one of the most fun areas of gaming culture: cosplay.

Cosplay is a combination of the words *costume* and *play*. The basic idea is pretty simple: dress up like your favorite video game character. But people who take cosplay seriously devote huge amounts of time to making incredible costumes. Cosplay experts must learn how to sew, use a wide variety of materials, apply makeup, and even work with metal or wood. They share tips with fellow cosplayers online while working on these elaborate costumes. When they've finished, they can show off their completed costumes online or at gamer gatherings.

Some cosplayers create costumes just to have fun. Others enter competitions. Judges decide which person looks most like the character he or she is trying to imitate. They may also award prizes for things like the best weapon or the best armor. Competitions are usually held at places like video game trade shows or even movie and TV conventions. At these events, people dressed as video game characters can mingle and chat with people dressed as characters from movies or TV shows. They're probably the only place you'll ever see Mario eating a hamburger with Batman and a Power Ranger.

Cosplayers dress up as characters from games, movies, comics, books, and TV shows.

GAMING WEB SERIES

Since before the dawn of YouTube, gamers have used Internet videos to comment on video game culture. Oh yeah—and they also use it to ruthlessly make fun of their favorite games.

One popular way to create gaming videos for the web is through the use of machinima. Machinima combines the words *machine* and *cinema*. Basically, it means people using video games as cheap and easy ways to make animated movies. One of the most popular machinima series, *Red vs. Blue*, is made using Microsoft's popular *Halo* series. Here's how it works. The creators

Red vs. Blue connect their Xboxes and start a multiplayer game. They each have a script telling them when to move, jump, or take any other action. Meanwhile, one of the players is basically acting as the camera, using his or her point of view to look at what the other players are doing. The camera player's screen is recorded to make the video. Finally, funny voice-overs are recorded to match what's happening on the screen.

Many of the jokes in *Red vs. Blue* make fun of things in shooting games that hard-core gamers would be familiar with. For example, in one episode, two characters argue about comically unimportant things, such as who will get the sniper rifle with the cool scope.

Red vs. Blue has proved to be hugely popular with gamers. The series of videos started in 2003, and it is still going today. Microsoft has even asked the creators of the series to make videos for special company events.

Michael "Burnie" Burns, *right*, one of the creators of *Red vs. Blue*, talks about machinima at a 2013 festival.

The cast of *The Guild* signs autographs at a video game convention in 2011.

Another popular web series that comments on gaming culture is *The Guild*. The show is a live-action comedy series about a guild that plays an online game together. They play a game similar to real games like *World of Warcraft*. The series, which began in 2007, has a large, devoted fan base.

Much of *The Guild's* popularity can be attributed to its creator and star, actress Felicia Day. She had previously appeared in shows such as *Buffy the Vampire Slayer*. She is also a big gamer. This is important, because it means she can use *The Guild* to accurately comment on gaming culture. Day realized that many people think of gamers as always being male, and she wanted to show that stereotypical idea is not always true.

stereotypical =
a belief that is simplified and widely held

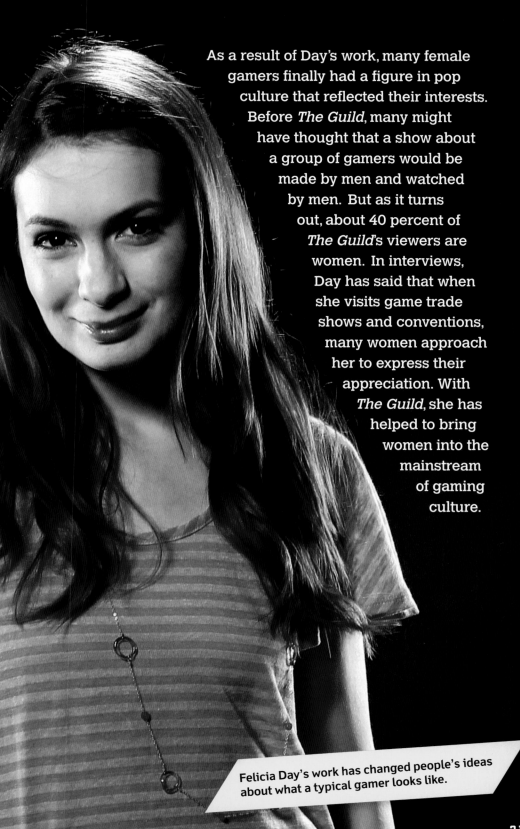

As a result of Day's work, many female gamers finally had a figure in pop culture that reflected their interests. Before *The Guild*, many might have thought that a show about a group of gamers would be made by men and watched by men. But as it turns out, about 40 percent of *The Guild*'s viewers are women. In interviews, Day has said that when she visits game trade shows and conventions, many women approach her to express their appreciation. With *The Guild*, she has helped to bring women into the mainstream of gaming culture.

Felicia Day's work has changed people's ideas about what a typical gamer looks like.

GAMING TV SHOWS:
Games on the Small Screen

Turning on your favorite game console isn't the only way to get your gaming fix on a TV. Gaming television shows have been around for decades. There are two basic kinds of these shows. One kind takes place within the world of a video game and tells new stories. The other features people discussing video games.

Most of the shows that take place in a video game series have been cartoons. For example, *Pokémon* started off as a Game Boy game before it turned into a smash-hit TV show. After the game came out in 1996, the show followed in 1997. And more than 750 episodes later, it's still going strong.

Not all video game shows have been so successful. Back in the late 1980s, TV networks were trying to make money off the amazing popularity of video games. One result was *The Super Mario Bros. Super Show!* The show was part live-action and part animated, and it didn't end up having very much to do with the actual games themselves.

The Super Mario Bros. Super Show! lasted from September to December 1989.

Bizarrely, Mario was played by a professional wrestler in the live-action parts.

By the 2000s, TV producers realized that gamers wanted more than just cartoons. With this in mind, the TV network G4 was launched in 2002. G4 featured several shows about video games. People discussed games, reviewed them, shared gaming tips and tricks, and more. The network saw success for a while, but it soon became clear that gamers preferred going to the Internet for their video game information. The network removed most of its gaming shows in 2013, replacing them with shows about travel, cooking, and fashion.

This Ain't No Game...

SUPER MARIO BROS. THE MOVIE

With the incredible graphics of today, many modern games look practically like movies. The only difference? You can control video games. But it's important to remember that video games didn't always look so good. You would think that video game movies would have been popular back when game graphics weren't so good. And you'd be right. Unfortunately, most of those movies have been terrible.

One of the most notorious video game movies of all time was *Super Mario Bros.* Released in 1993, it was a total disaster. For one thing, it was just downright weird. One of the enemies from the *Mario* games was called a Goomba. It was a little brown mushroom creature that ran around. Sounds weird enough already, right? But the makers of the *Super Mario Bros.* movie turned Goombas into strange, tall creatures that stood on two legs, wore spiky suits, and had half-dinosaur, half-human heads. Whoa.

Most video game movies, from *Mortal Kombat* to *Resident Evil* to *Max Payne*, have been hated by critics. However, video game movies aren't all bad news. One recent movie about video game culture was much more successful. The 2012 animated movie *Wreck-It Ralph* takes place inside the worlds of many different video games. Although the main characters were made up for the movie, they interact with characters that many players know and love, such as Sonic the Hedgehog and Pac-Man. Both critics and audiences loved the movie.

Wreck-It Ralph included tons of references to old games as well as new ones.

GAMING COMICS:
Graphic Novels with Great Graphics

When you think about comic books, you probably think about the characters that got their start there: Batman, Superman, and SpiderMan. But if you're a gamer, you should add Sonic the Hedgehog to that list.

Video games and comics have been a great fit together. For one thing, video games and comic books often involve similar subject matter, such as soldiers, super heroes, aliens, robots, and magical fantasy worlds. Also, many comic book writers and artists have worked in gaming over the decades. There's a lot of crossover between the gaming and comics communities. So it shouldn't be a big surprise that there have been numerous popular comic books

One of the most successful is *Sonic the Hedgehog*. Published by Archie Comics, the *Sonic* comic has been around since 1992. That makes it the longest-running comic book series based on a video game. The *Sonic* comic rewards readers who have enjoyed the series for a long time, setting up plot developments and then having them pay off in interesting ways in later issues.

Another video game comic found success because it filled in the blanks between the games in a series. That comic is *Gears of War*, based on the games of the same name. The games feature a team of soldiers with futuristic weapons fighting an alien invasion. Because most of the game is spent running around turning aliens into puddles of goo, there isn't much time for the story. This is where the *Gears of War* comic came in. It told readers about what happened to the characters between games in the series. Although it only ran for twenty-four issues, the series gave fans a chance to explore the *Gears of War* universe.

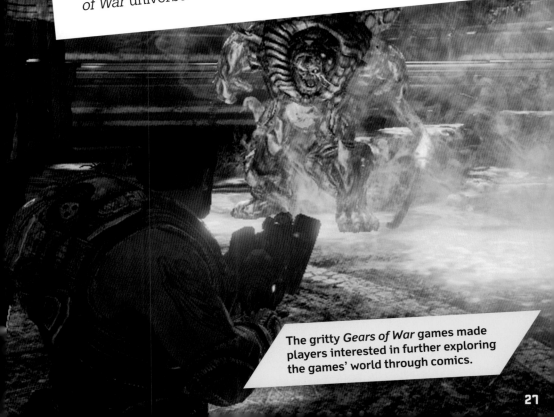

The gritty *Gears of War* games made players interested in further exploring the games' world through comics.

KEY DATES IN GAMING CULTURE

1939: The earliest example of cosplay. Science fiction author Forrest J. Ackerman wears a costume to the First World Science Fiction Convention in New York.

1989: *The Super Mario Bros. Super Show!* begins airing on TV, disappointing Mario fans everywhere.

1992: The first *Sonic the Hedgehog* comic comes out. More than 250 issues later, the series is still going.

1993: The *Super Mario Bros.* movie comes out. Fans of the *Super Mario Bros.* games fear the series is ruined forever.

1995: The first E3 is held, kicking off a series of trade shows that excite gamers every year.

1997: The *Pokémon* TV series begins, spawning more than 750 episodes and more than a dozen movies.

2002: Xbox Live is launched, bringing online console gaming into the mainstream.

2003: *Red vs. Blue*, a web series that makes fun of games while using them as a cheap animation tool, is created.

2007: *The Guild* web series begins, helping to disprove stereotypes about games and gamers.

2008: The *Gears of War* comics pull gamers deeper into the *Gears of War* universe when they're not busy battling hordes of alien foes.

2012: *Wreck-It Ralph*, one of the first video game movies that fans actually liked, comes out.

2013: *Wreck-It Ralph* is nominated for the Academy Award for Best Animated Feature.

E3 Expo
http://www.e3insider.com
Because the general public can't get into the E3 trade show, check out this site for an inside look at the awesome games and game creators at the show.

Kaplan, Arie. *The Epic Evolution of Video Games.* Minneapolis: Lerner Publications, 2014.
Have you ever wondered what video games would be like if they never changed? Take a look at how video games have evolved over the years, and learn about the kinds of games we might be playing in the future.

Killzone Intercept **Q&A**
http://blog.us.playstation.com/2012/11/15/killzone-intercept-qa-fighting-the-helghast-on-film
Want to learn more about the *Killzone Intercept* fan film? Then read this interview with the film's creator, who explains how it took two years to produce fourteen minutes of film.

Plunkett, Luke. *How the World's Biggest LAN Party Is Built*
http://kotaku.com/5962826/how-the-worlds-largest-lan-party-is-built
Check out photos from Dreamhack Winter, a massive LAN party held in Sweden. More than ten thousand gamers showed up at the 2012 event.

Sonic the Hedgehog **Comics**
http://www.comicvine.com/sonic-the-hedgehog/49-11074
Interested in learning more about *Sonic* comics? On this site, you can browse through every issue of the long-running comic series.

Tassi, Paul. *The 10 Steps to Becoming a Pro Gamer*
http://www.forbes.com/sites/insertcoin/2012/03/30/the-10-steps-to-becoming-a-pro-gamer
So you want to become a professional gamer? Read this article to figure out how to get started.

Ten Video Game Movie Disasters
http://games.yahoo.com/blogs/plugged-in/10-video-game-movie-disasters-223058191.html
Want to learn more about truly awful video game movies? Check out this list of some of the worst.

PHOTO ACKNOWLEDGMENTS

The images in this book are used with the permission of: © PRNewsFoto/Nintendo/ AP Images, p. 4; © PolkaDot/Getty Images/JupiterImages/ThinkStock, p. 5; © Marvin Joseph /The Washington Post/Getty Images, pp. 6, 10; © Blizzard/dapd/AP Images, p. 7; © Joerg Sarbach/AP Images, p. 8; © Waltraud Grubitzsch/picture-alliance/dpa/ AP Images, p. 9; © Derek Bauer/AP Images for Blizzard, p. 11; © Barone Firenze/AP Images, pp. 12, 13, 29; © Ditty_about_summer/Shutterstock Images, p. 14; © David McNew/Getty Images, p. 15; © Jose Gil/Shutterstock Images, p. 16; © Pamela Joe McFarlane/iStockphoto, p. 17; © Microsoft/dapd/AP Images, p. 18; © Rita Quinn/Getty Images for SXSW, p. 19; © Derek Bauer/AP Images for Blizzard, p. 20; © Matt Sayles/ AP Images, p. 21; © TV Tokyo image/Sankei Shimbun/AP Images, p. 22; © DiC Enterprises/Everett Collection, p. 23; © Buena Vista/Everett Collection, p. 24; © Disney/AP Images, p. 25; © Keith Srakocic/AP Images, p. 26; © Microsoft/AP Images, p. 27; © Vlad Turchenko/Shutterstock Images, p. 28.

Front cover: © Antonio Jodice/Dreamstime.com.

Main body text set in Calvert MT Std Regular 11/16.
Typeface provided by Monotype Typography.